NO DOUBT I
WILL RETURN
A DIFFERENT
MAN

NO DOUBT I
WILL RETURN
A DIFFERENT
MAN

Tobias Wray

Cleveland State University Poetry Center
Cleveland, Ohio

ISBN: 978-1-7348167-1-6

First edition

23   22   21   20   19   5   4   3   2   1

This book is published by the Cleveland State University Poetry Center,
2121 Euclid Avenue, Cleveland, Ohio 44115-2214
www.csupoetrycenter.com and is distributed by
SPD / Small Press Distribution, Inc. www.spdbooks.org.

Cover image: Maxfield Parrish, *The Lantern Bearers*, 1908, oil on canvas mounted on board, 40 x 32 in. Chrystal Bridges Museum of American Art, Bentonville, Arkansas, 2006.71. Photography by Dwight Primiano.
Cover design: Amy Freels
No Doubt I Will Return a Different Man was designed and typeset by Amy Freels in Adobe Garamond Pro with Mr. Eaves Sans display.

A catalog record for this title is available from the Library of Congress.

Contents

*They have hung
lanterns in the branches.*

*It is unclear which if any
is the moon.*

ALL THE GRAND DEATHS

Death by snapping vine,
death by cat o' nines, by dole,
by virtue or grace; by mistake.

Death by heroic lace
left too long by the window;
death by 1983, by augury.

Death by wingspan, by
the lengths to which you'll go.
Death by island, by shoal.

Scene: *A father and son driving.*
    MAN:
    ME: Yes, I am.
    Car stops.
    MAN:

Death by wellspring,
by being
too much of anything.

Death by lesson, by reach,
by thoughtless breach, by loosening wind
on a shining beach.

Scene: *On a dock by a lake.*
     BOY:
     ME: Why me?
     BOY:

     under the dock (death
     by firefly light); *teeth* (death
     by flickering), *tongue*
     without end
     ME:

Death by tides, by dunes.
By doorway, by feigning. Death by
maze, by ripple-split moon; by cocoon.

Scene: *Outside the bar, a group of men*
     surround him.
     FIRST MAN:
     Throws a punch.
     ME:
     throws him
     down (death

     by subduction), *throws*
     the other against the wall—

     SECOND MAN: *cries out* (death's
abbreviation)

FIRST MAN:
(death by gavel, by paddle)
ME: *against his ear*
Love's forty dark ships
close in.

Death by missing bridge,
death by hinge, by lozenge.
Death by fringe, by bondage.
Death by head over heels.
Death by rolling
down steep hills.

Scene: *A couple of queers*
    on a slick-black street,
    in and out
    of pooling light.

    BOY: *in between ragged breaths, ragged*
    hands What do you
    want?

    ME:
    (death by awe,
    by raw, open maw).

Death by noon, by
whatever the fuck, by horseshoe toss;
by unread signal, a penny, heads-up.

Death by reckoning, by beckoning.

Scene: *A lamplit room,*
            his son's final letter
            on the table.
            MAN:

            His eye holds the page
            like the last note of a hymn,
            what could have been.

            He returns it to its creases,
            letting each line extend.

However much is left
is left adrift, memory
as apogee, hosanna, death

by odyssey,
by modesty. All of us, yes,
drifting, two-by-two,
in wider and wider arcs.

THE DUSK

I wish I were as certain as the dusk
that has seen queers slip down the stairs
for a tête-à-tête with some old queen,

tattoo of a ruler along his arm
with 8" at the tip. This turnstile start
to his theme park ride. Or the priestly spouses

who thump cantaloupe in the market and sniff
the Jurassic husks of pineapple,
while stars vie for those burlesque

thighs of sunset. That last dipping inch.
I'll be certain as the dusk. Let truth be a gong
hung, like God, stiff and dumb. Let it be

still as a parked car and nothing like the dawn
that spools out bright strings like blood,
and we, the sharks, turning at the light.

THE HIDDEN CHOIR

Some questions promise to return everything to fire.
True archetypes, fathers. The fields sing their insect song, wanting more.

My father, an ancient grammar. Call this a study of men,
of their soft necessity, insurance against them. I remember dandelions

blown across yards filled with hidden choirs. We survived
thanks to those archipelagos whose patterns turned to seamless arabesques.

I'll tell you what happened. Meaning is made from the telling: old damage
comes alive behind the eyes. The evening's buzz grows quiet there,

a dim pool we are almost swimming. Practical poets, astronomers gave *nebulae,*
the word for clouds, to the filmy graves of supernovaed stars. Flung out now,

a future matter: nothing made can be lost—it is banked. It is important to say this:
there is more we can become. Caught in that cotton-candy-maker pull, until

hot, hot, hot, another nursery for the blaze of noons. For years, my father
was all we talked about, until we untethered that song from its source, flung it out.

Some questions become mirrors. Such delicate codes, we hitch
a ride with soft necessity. This is what we can become. A deer's tail

flickers behind a sapling on this impossible shore, and I try to imagine
what the shape of this lake is like: a bird taking flight or a child running behind
    the house.

TURING'S THEORIES REGARDING HOMOSEXUALITY

If anything, we are this: hive, industry, insistent tales of fairy rings, all-chemical, penetrable, snow-drifted, darkling, that evening Murray stopped me outside the show, the amber of bourbon, windblown, sigil, lips tight, diurnal, lockstep, some future Velcro, conjured to the door, the way he took my hat and my platitudes, inserting look, opening, breaking open, knocking impatiently, clever sleight, clever ruse, standing by the window, weak blue like approaching light, clean, brandishing, he wanted us to have tea, leafy green, over-flowery, air, mist, he said he wanted to talk to a real scientist, entryway, hairline, disorganized, slick fabrications, the black line we ignore between speaking lips, eclipse, angles, blitzed, top to bottom, he held me in his hand like a kiss, Panama-brimmed, blinking, circuitry-sawing, sweating, the safest way to convey is from behind, lantern bearers, the word *water* in French, turbines, turbines waking up, the open-ask, how to subtract the man from his signs, his wide smile like a bridge to paradise, nightstands, the swell of morning behind heavy curtains, all those collections of O's, archipelagos, like planetary accretions, this swirling in, we press to spread wide, swallowed, discordant, gravity's only compromise, yes, relentlessly pressed, spreading, I opened, uncomplicated, unacknowledged, that the last time must needs remain memory, staccato of no applause, shoes on walls, fabric, bruise, a blast, helix-like in irony, fabulous liquids, his face increases in detail daily, unrevealable, that low smell of him.

I began to look at him as if he'd given something
he didn't intend to let me keep.

Woodchips on his workshop floor—
the bones of waves,

a throbbing graveyard.

PANTHALASSA, THE UNIVERSAL SEA

His own father's funeral, the first we'd seen of him in seven years,
was the day my father asked us to bury all grievance, his voice swollen,

a bulwark cracked sidelong and jagged. The sounds to which
you abandon a ship. Once, there was no separation:

the land stretched forever, a great sea held all of the forever
after that. My father seemed undriftable, committed, before distance

became obsession. Once blurred, anything could be a pleasure. Perhaps
we all return to that great expanse, the chromatic glaze of waves.

Our search for consonance complete once distance
gains its choral glistening. But here, whatever is left only slides apart.

The coffin still waiting for its earth, we returned to the car.
The road beyond the cemetery gate cut into irregular shapes, same as the sky.

QUEEN SAMSON

And in your city, I held my feast.
And in your city, I gathered men great in number.
I tore ladders from the walls in your city.
And in your city, I full force bested.
I tore the walls from their sitting.

And in your city, I held my feast.
And in your city, I took men to my chamber.
And in their city, I full force bested.
I rent their clothes, I broke their walls, and in your city
I cast fire where it needed to burn,
and in your city, I howled my name in reverse.

The people of this city have familiar faces.
Tragedy, anciently composed:
the gravest, most moral and profitable.
For the love of building, of burning.

And in your city, feasts
and in your city, great in slumber
and in your city,

walls, once broken, recall
without end their powers
of division revisited. To hold
this thing we care about
we name it with a myth.

BUGGERY

What is history if not a story full of holes?
>*Sex between men*
>*was illegal in parts of the UK*
>*until 1982. These proceedings provide vibrant*
>*and detailed evidence of the worlds of London's*
>*historical homosexuals.*

At his, the curtains drawn.
But the next day, uniforms at the door:
the air gummed like cold
blood. We'll swing
like prisms from a chandelier.
>*Until 1861, all penetrative*
>*homosexual acts committed*
>*were punishable by death.*
>*Then, hanging was replaced by life imprisonment, and after*
>*the passage of the Labouchere Amendment, by up to two years'*
>*incarceration. Some chose chemical castration.* The animal smell
persists on the surface
of a scoured body. We fuck ourselves
full of holes. He, like an angel. Are these men
my fathers? Oh, how the body persists.
What legacy, what long computation.
>*To prove sodomy one needed*
>*at least two eyewitnesses*
>*and evidence of both penetration*
>*and ejaculation. As a result*
>*most trials in the Proceedings*
>*are for the lesser offense of*
>*assault with sodomitical intent.*

For the sake of symmetry,
diagonal to the window, like a poem.
Bent over, his ass was an apple
cut in half. The whole fruit bears no threat—only this
interior flesh, its intent; the stem pulled
through and out. *We are only awake on the inside*, he
bathes the holes with promises, with future dates and time: you
I will fill, you I will fling down, fling into, flee.

> *From then, what is known about behaviors*
> *and attitudes within these communities*
> *can be found mostly through trials*
> *of blackmail. Otherwise, for all intents*
> *and purposes,*
>
> > *this world did not exist.*

WEAK BONDS

are those forces of attraction, like gravity,
that do not take much energy

to break. Was this why you held me
the way a branch holds fruit, so lightly,

the squeeze seems to push?

Some moments dare to gather
all of history in miniature. I too am one

throbbing star in a jar and begin to roll
off every table. Fruit grows sweeter

after the drop.

All eye where the stem was cut.
Don't talk to me about rot, don't you dare

breathe a word. A dirigible unmoored,
I couldn't care.

I'll swim in air.

FALSE SPRING FOR TELEMACHUS

In waiting for my father, I became his son:
a man waiting for something to happen.

We thought we knew what it needed to be.

Any moment now, blue hammers
will tumble from the sky.

It is hard to be a son.

Believing they know what time it is,
gardens wake in late-winter birth months.

The air warm, they take up the invitation of light.

Did you know
the colder the environment, the longer you live
and the slower you move? Greenland sharks

shift their shadows under the ice belly for hundreds of years—

shadows bent toward depth. A room bends
over the eye. Nature's nature
being conflict,

I worry the outcome like a sore.

Did you know
the sun sets blue on Mars?
Holograms, so lovely in the night. The familiar,
so inviting to trust.

Finding my father, I almost forgave him.

Meaningless and magnified, the love song's
radial stroke. Every decision

fathered what-ifs. Thirsty, green mouths
scream like a crime,
calling out in supplication, for sublimation.

Maybe it will be different this time.
Already, they can hear it, death's long rhyme.

TURING TESTED

Such queer things, elegies.

All shapes have a beginning,
Turing supposed: morphogenesis. It is this initial
spinning that describes us, our original moan,
developed from spiral and signal—notion

of a physical soul.

Popcorn strung on a string. We are heroic machines,
pushed out from DNA center, designed
to pull back curtains from their windows,
to make trains go, to sing.

Wars hold strange words in their teeth,
in the submarine's deep.

For every eye, a lid. For every war,
a shiny new machine.

Seagulls dipped behind government
buildings like blips on radar screens. Slow, unsteady.
He first met Murray outside the Regal Cinema.
Murray just out of *Monkey Business*,
starring Cary Grant, Ginger Rogers,
Marilyn Monroe. Turing saw *The Snows of Kilimanjaro*,
and in fact, it did snow. It snowed and snowed.

They had afternoon tea the next day,
leaves left drifting into their knots, water into shadow.

Before there were Homosexuals
there were Contrary Sensations.
The undeserving streets awaited
their soldiers, saviors.

A genius of solution, he imagined
a test for whether man or man-thing.
Genius, for all its solitude,

means *a fathering force,*
attendant spirit.

He was at work on mathematical biology
to ascertain origin's shape
when he fell for a hustler named Murray.

Loved him, maybe.
Or, if not love, perhaps
they exchanged some other code.
Nothing made should be lost,
one can hear him explain.

Gross indecency. Section 11.
Convicted in March,
a month of caws and echoes.

Bad jokes can kill, he must have laughed
from his cell. Robed men in wigs offered judgment:
selection. He chose chemical castration

over prison. A flood
through narrow cracks.
The pressure of walls inside veins.

Injections of stilboestrol,
a hormone treatment designed
to produce impotence. The give
of the skin on the arm as the needle
slid in: *No doubt I will return
a different man*, he said.

The treatments caused
his breasts to grow. All things
change: another law to weaponize.

He loved *Snow White*, loved
the novelty of animation, dream-haze
come to life. A woman lifts her arm to singing branches,
pure song: what integration, what connection.
He was in awe of novelty, where
it might go. His eyes wide

as a queen dipped her apple
in its brutal brew. In the mirror,
he saw all the world could be
one remarkable machine.

Those wind-swept government halls,
the appeal of uniforms, corridors,
secrets tucked into pockets with pens
and keys. Small words, like *launch*,
slender as their fingers over the keys.

Turing broke every code,
unexploded a thousand ships.

Then, guilty of being
decrypted. Faulted for lying on a couch
after afternoon tea. For plucking something
from the string and holding it in his mouth
for an hour after tea. The exhaustive brevity
of opinion. Their eyes squinted

in disgust, unassailable decision.
He understood the limits
of what they could perceive.

His housekeeper found him
stiff from cyanide, waiting for nothing.
He was a man of habit. Evenings,
he would have an apple
before sleep. *One bite and all your dreams...*
It was not unusual for it to be found at his bedside,
half-eaten, his housekeeper said. See?

Teeth mark windows to the core:
the dark wink of what could only be a seed.

So, it rises like a bruise,
this empty room.

I bury my hands inside
bones that look like you.

BEGINNING'S END

I remember the shower's dim light—his skin,
the color of memory when it has no sense of what it is.
The burgeoning reality of touch as wet skin,

knowing it as impossible—the problem of a boy seeing
a man's skin as skin is that it becomes what it is,
like a sculpture suddenly breathing. I remember

my father in the shower, and remember
his watching my watching, and every encounter
with every man thereafter was nameable. And me,

toweling off in shock, someone having seen something
I hadn't. The blossoming of being
seen and seeing. I remember the yard swimming uncut

down to our landlord's fishing pond, the baseball field,
the rope swing twisting. I remember the grass

jumping, late-day buzz strung all over the trees.
There were so many more insects then.

EACH OF US CHIMERA

Soon after he came home to Arkansas,
mother's cousin Larry became a stone on a hill.
She tells of the monkey leashed

and taught to ride his shoulder
as he walked the couple blocks to Main
when they were young, the sixties. They didn't

know each other well, but my mother shows me,
as we drive by his old house,
where the big cage would rest,

there, and she tells me how the cotton drifted
like snow into brightening ditches
up and down every street. I imagine

a white-faced capuchin, a pirate's pet,
with a smart red vest. She spins
and I retrieve the memories. I ask her

anything—the old names of mountains
and saints, how to stay awake,
how her cousin Larry died, and the others,

how she thinks the world thinks. She tells me
and I remember. We creatures of the small
and yet collective. Our understanding

shimmers like schools of thought, glinting
as it turns. She says she never suspected
me. That I would have this

avuncular need. Larry, too, my original: how
some gay men say *family* to mean refuge,
refutation. I needed to imagine him,

to see his end. The flat and unsurprisingly plain
stone, lain next to Eulah and Oren. Beyond
sentiment, *July, 1989*: nothing to do

with AIDS, nothing to do
with ghosts, those flimsy fads, nothing to do
with wanting someone to have gone before

and come back. Even epitaphs can lose
their certainty. He died before we ever met,
but I wanted to touch what remained,

to keep the conversation ever approaching.
Visiting from Milwaukee, my ex noticed
so many of the markers read *UNKNOWN*.

Older than me, he'd never seen that before.
The first thing he did back at the car
was gasp dramatically. What?

Looking at his phone, he said Carole King
had died. But it was a hoax. She lives
somewhere in Idaho. Someone once told me

gay men have become a commercial
for themselves. But I thought we were done
buying that bullshit. Look,

something is owed. If we must be both,
adjective and suffix, let us go before
and come back. They say

fetal genetic material
migrates to a mother's brain and remains
postpartum, reprogramming connections.

Some mirrors have more questions.
They say time, too, listens from behind.
At almost seventy, Mom lives

in event afterglow. No one's story is over, yet
half our family has fit
back into the earth, into its endless holes.

We try to make them proud.
It was a rhesus, she corrects me.
A rhesus monkey,

she says after reading this. He kept it
in a chicken-wire cage and carried it
around town on his shoulder.

That was when the cotton gin
was still going, gave the streets and the air
a certain quality, wispy. Mom said

he didn't have the same energy
she was used to feeling from other
men. He was missing something,

neutral, flicked off or... Her father
asked her what she thought of him, fishing
for some confirmation, she figured. There were

questions when he died. She said
that he was different, said she didn't
know. I like to think of him that way,

impossible to know. We are in the process
of a certain unraveling, as if the past
exploded and this is the sense

the parts have made. I ask her anyway,
our understanding glinting as it turns.
Let this be why he came home,

not to die but to recombine. Cotton
lining every ditch, she said,
like something torn apart.

LANIAKEA, THE IMMEASURABLE HEAVENS

Father, I forget when you went off to war and never returned,
though there was never peace after that. Or you left to deal
with a warring heart and returned once or twice, father,

though I forget. I forget the way you pulled us in,
asked us to make you bigger than you were. As I pan out,
looking back, what mendacious symmetry: I am beyond you now;

bigger. And older, I forget not to tell your stories: the mildewed carpets
of your beat-up pickup, how you insisted we listen to jazz on long drives,
how Lake Pontchartrain held all manner of creatures I could only imagine,
how they must have swum in wide circles as we drove by.

HEAVY CURTAINS

He left, we were done, forgive us. We didn't consider sleep our
identity, yet we lived in the dark. The position of our hands, an
elegy—our feet, tombstone glyphs. Now, we ask for memory,
wince at blood: this old story, magnified, lit like snow. The truth
is cold: eventually, we learned he went after a little girl. When
we lived at the parsonage, during his first tenure-track teaching
gig. Such facts, the corpse of an insect trapped behind light
fixture glass, uncertain and bright. A sudden smudge. She's still
uncovering details with a trauma therapist. My god. It is best to
engage memory's bloody war than to run away. Right? It is
better than erasing what my father has done. Such futures insist
on rearranging the past—the forgotten smudge suddenly
twitches.

Best to accept what we now have: why
he placed our hearts in a box; why he needed to bury it in the dark.

SOME BROKEN COLOSSUS

We are   beyond ruined temples;
if sons may claim   those with whom

they will begin   I must have fucked up

the prayer
by no luck   landed here

his final expression   the shoulder
of a tree turned   against its shadow

a plume of smoke from a dropped match
in bare-tree woods   far from camp

We are a book whose perfect spine
has never been cracked

a feather   stuck
to the bottom   of a truck
torn at by wind   what the fuck
happened to   him

TURING IN THE GARDEN HUMMING BACH

The crushed path leads out, leads back.
I have spent my life in pieces small as pennies,

a concerto's worth of teeth and tongue, bridge
and throat. Scents gather their loose sleeves—

peonies, redolent of fireworks in a fog.
His love like reptilian eyes, folds

flecked and wet. A bouquet whose failing slits
fall wide and spent: no doubt, I am happy.

Lighthouses cast back out to sea.
They will find you the way

skin finds skin, over and over again,
leaving the same as they came.

THE LAMENT OF ICARUS

My father was a man made miserable
by a more masterful son. He's a musician, but I loved best
his cherrywood sculpture of dancing bears chained
to a stake. I have it still—a testament, given
how I move. One, in a Parrish blue hat,
circles the other in my every living room, entranced,
as a wistful circus ring rises at their feet. Clumsy
and leaden, their chains are tucked behind them.

When I first encountered Draper's *Icarus*, the first
painting I ever loved, I recognized the pose
and attempted to cut a woodblock copy of my own.
I wanted him, to be like him but with eyelids waking, so I took
a blade and cut slender punctuations. What struck me
were his wings—tremendous, strong, hardly melted at all.
As though *lament* meant nothing at all.

After so much time, he might still fly: I lifted each feather
with fine, deep gouges.

MUSIC ARISES FROM COMPONENT PARTS OR THE DREAM OF A CLARINET

Once done,
my father pulled
the instrument apart.
Mouthpiece, barrel.
Joint by joint,
until the bell, wide
as a mouth singing
or screaming,
lay like a dried-up

fountain, a fountain
wet only at the rim
where the last notes
shone still. We were safe
while he practiced:
that music, almost
pattern. The sound
of a clarinet: reedy
absence. He would wave,

as he played,
the black scepter slowly
as if the moment
were stuck in glint,
a spell that never held.

Fires lit under
soon-to-empty trees
bounced sparks
against razor-wire stars.

Like a single voice
that beckons to fairy-tale
children, a voice they know
as ancient, dangerous,
yet somehow made of gold.

It took me years
to recall what I heard then.
More than unclear warning, or
loggia in lapsed light.

Anywhere in the house,
we his audience, sunk
like walking stones
over water, trapped
in fading song and after.

My sister tells me
we hid in the closet,
his hard face. Is there
anything more sinister
than a memory lost?
Than a bare music stand?

POSTCARDS

1.
By the time we arrived in Montpellier, the evening
was the perfect anti-brochure.

Sex workers worked the corner
in torn stockings and flowing wigs,

admirably glaring clientele down
under the aqueduct that cradled weeds

in every fissure like a protest
against use or some truce with Nature.

We sang to a drunk, captive moon,
balanced like cats on the Opera's roof.

2.
In the early aughts, we still needed
to be everything, camped around the kitchen table

my impromptu French family
perpetrating incest so cinematically.

La Club villa rose rose neon on the beach
with rooms where men danced in cages

and curtains drawn so whoever could suck
whomever off. I liked the big rocks

piled near the surf, how they dared you to climb up,
how salt stung in the formidable wind.

3.

I once consulted the stars
but can't recall their wisdom.

Was it like love? No, it flickered,
never flared. It was its own affair.

So many snails in the courtyard after a rain,
the path crackled as we walked.

The stars, with all their hints of shatter,
don't deal in specifics. Those were the days

we drove through Napoleon's lanes, the long
accordions of afternoon letting us tune them.

4.
La Licorne and *Les Trois grâces*, bright fountains
lit for a night downtown. You stepped

into the water, pants tugged up to your thigh.
I kept watch for cops and made

a note to be more like you. *I have been*
in all your movies, and spoke all my parts

like an evangelist, and kissed
like an astronomer the liquid curves of your distance,

we sang to a drunk, captive moon,
balanced like cats on the Opera's roof.

CAMERA, FIELD

In the photograph, the buck stares back.
From a little distance, the quick-steeple gesture
of one raised leg. Such stillness,

only permanent until. Suspended in gaze,
the photographer is the real subject,
and watches being watched, notices

the watching. The buck is more than curious,
his rack held to chandelier height. His ears,
his neck bear the moment the way a bridge

bears gravity. Bent against this
or any hunt,
the buck decides when

the cowbirds, under their own graces,
ready to climb
into the field of sky.

The image cruises
a simple science:
all chase, all escape.

IN THE NAME OF THE FATHER

Or the last dream from last night:
how, out of spite, my father kept me in a wooden cage.
What is your name? Nobody. Why am I here?

I tried to wake in the mornings, to reach
the book on his table, but after much strain
a new question folded over every sentence,

lines of verse turned to a cypher
for the dead language of distant seas. He was always
coming down the stairs, ever approaching.

I hatched a plan to blind him and escape:
how he would scream and crash onto the bars,
breaking them like sticks, how I would retrieve his keys.

Nothing went as planned. I missed his eye
and cut off his head. It rolled against the far wall
and never looked away again.

SNOW WHITE

The glass coffin has handles of old wood smooth as bone. Overhead, a tree bows over
the sleeping face—a man in a dressing gown. You study his neck, where it climbs down
under the collar—the direction by which
a man is described. The man in the glass coffin sighs.
Recognition, a leafy green.
You look closer to see the fine breath rise between slightly parted lips. His
two hands lay like rocks.
Now, the glass is fogged, nearly overcome by sleep. You reach to clean it

with your breath, with your please, before remembering
you are outside, closer to the familiar tree.
This must make you some kind of royalty.
Birdsong has come on. Male voices gently rise in chant from behind the hill. Perhaps
they are going to war. War,
the color of concrete. The man is full of dreaming, his eyes eating cake behind his lids.

SONATA FOR ONE CLARINET BY JOHN CAGE

Scene: *A near-empty stage before the concert,*
the musician, like a lonely god,
plays off-center to a circle of light.

No nest to empty, no nest to warm.
Birds are such old dinosaurs, and beasts
go down in shrill winter. More than
protection the shell wants breaking.
To grow old, inimitable. How some fathers

walk the world wide, thinking
their children will never know
such elegance, will shatter
what they have.

CLARINETIST: This mic is wrong. It should
go left. There. Okay, I'll run through
the Cage first, and then we'll see
what needs tightening. *He seems unsure;*
there is no answer. At the last note,
the empty stage exhales.

This is the way each piece is played,
pained, emptied like glass. If art reflects life,
art is a shell. He scatters the shards like notes
to time. Only celebration
remains. Something to invite
the empty seats to weep, the balconies to kneel.

HOW THE SHADOWS ARE

nothing without the headlights to guide them,
though their edges glare too bright, how
like a finger over a small flame
or nail, the pain you can see coming
is the one you wanted, and we dared to be young,
wandered drunk into the street, begging to be shot,
but I got up even after the gun struck my open mouth,
after the men who looked too young, lonely enough
to be gods, who took away the night, the men
who never knew that after
I couldn't find my glasses, the ones
I spent too much on, the missing chip of tooth,
thought they must be there somewhere in the street,
a kind of forgiveness, how the rest of the story runs
like veins shot from headlights through the trees.

KEEPING THE FENCE

We used to walk the line sacking beer cans
hunters had thrown on our side.
A childhood song, the rhythms of aluminum

muted in the jam-black garbage bag. The dry
switch-code of grass. We never asked
for what you would become. I can almost hear

the lowest clouds scuffed by those white pines
on the hill. A meadowlark startles.
There's a tyranny to the fence,

its weather-cracked posts,
its aching teeth strung against the wind.

The lake will freeze
into its long end-stop.

You taught mistakes.
I hear them carving into the waves.

THE QUESTIONS THEMSELVES

No one has called my sister in two days—we say the phone is dead
as though before it were alive. What it means to be alive

on the eve of destruction.
I too want to add the word *gently*.

Fever setting in, I once experienced a white-out
on a train in another country. People became a crowd of menacing wings,
the platform I collapsed onto
a sudden discotheque, hard and pavonine.

The fever lasted two days.
They too have a kind of life.

No one knows the origin of the question mark, but it seems obvious
that it is born of slipping. Some rooms have been built for this,
podiums and altars.

Some think it is owed to the shape of a cat's tail, or some kind of shorthand
for a word meaning *question*.

When she answers, I hope my sister's voice is the voice of someone who wants to live.

I PROPOSE TO RECONSIDER THE QUESTION

I.
Whether man or machine, my father loved us
like a scream in a hall. His ghost lingers on.
An essential question, like an eyehole.

>   Scene: *He takes my hand.*
>   MAN: Your loneliness
>   was a compass. Mine,
>   a masterpiece of war.
>
>   *The sound of scythes swinging,*
>   *or swans circling on water.*
>
>   ME: Every song
>   finds its throat. To call,
>   to choke. Answer
>   my question. *His hand*
>
>   *is gone. Wild rose bushes*
>   *burn in its place. Even his absence,*
>   *his silence: wild, requiring reaction.*

Someday, he will die.
When he dies, I will tell stories about islands.

II.
Every story fills with forty dark ships.

Of my father, I can tell you only this…

He isn't dead,
but I haven't seen him. Should I go looking?

What will I find? Loss leaves behind
invisible shadows, knowing the unseen
prefers to stay hidden.

> *From hidden speakers, somewhere above.*
> MACHINE: You may be hearing this
> for the first time, some chance map.
> This is how we grow
>
> *A machinic figure, Tragedy, descends in metallic gold,*
> *a chariot of levers in undulant motion. Tragedy*
> *slowly raises a hand, finger poised in the air.*
>
> past every limitation.

IN MY DREAM, TURING SHOWS ME
HIS GREATEST MACHINE

Turing and I fling ourselves
into a river black as a lake.
We kick, ungrapple, kick,
his hand heavier, pulling us down.
His hand clamped like a small
mandible over mine, my first jarring
attempt at diving; his aim, true.

We sling down to where
the machine, far below,
curries lights over the fanged weeds.
Like a flat, open palm, the mechanical bottom
seems to hold the river up.

We reach its circuited face
where the strands button off.
Turing tinkers with a panel,
his hands clawn, over-busy, his hands
the quietest thing above the lights.
From his work, bubbles
fury overhead, lit, then lost.
I lose time. He is there,

but then he is gone. He has flown
into some moment I wasn't attending,
leaving no instructions for proceeding.

How beauty, pith-like, sits
in the center of incomprehension.
This, his last machine, seems
to creature the blind dark, offering
anything that passes there long enough
its own set of eyes.

NOTES

The opening image (pg. 1) is an ekphrastic response to Maxfield Parrish's *The Lantern Bearers*, located at the Crystal Bridges Museum of American Art in Bentonville, Arkansas.

"All the Grand Deaths": The phrase "forty dark ships" comes from Homer's catalog of ships in *The Iliad*. Protesilaus sailed forty black ships to Troy and was the first to land there, and so the first to die in the Trojan War.

"The Dusk": This poem borrows its structure from W.B. Yeats's "The Dawn," which includes one of the greatest images in English-language poetry: "Above the cloudy shoulders of the horses." With thanks to Michael Heffernan for the inspiration.

"The Hidden Choir": The line "hot, hot, hot, another nursery for the blaze of noons" borrows from John Milton's last work, the closet drama *Samson Agonistes*. Milton's line is, "O dark, dark, dark, amid the blaze of noon..."

"Queen Samson": This poem is for Randall Mann, whose own "Colloquy between A and B" inspired it. Particularly the last lines: "But the world needs its fires, / its cities of shame."

"Tragedy, anciently composed: / the gravest, most moral and profitable," is again from *Samson Agonistes*, this time from Milton's introduction: "Tragedy, as it was antiently compos'd, hath been ever held the gravest, moralest, and most profitable of all other Poems: therefore said by Aristotle to be of power by raising pity and fear, or terror, to purge the mind of those and such like passions, that is to temper and reduce them to just measure with a kind of delight, stirr'd up by reading or seeing those passions well imitated."

"Buggery": The title references England's Buggery Act of 1533 and many of the subsequent lines borrow language from the Old Bailey court proceedings, London's criminal court, as well as other histories of English legal proceedings regarding sodomy laws. A few years after this poem was written and almost 500 years after the country's first civil sodomy law, legislation was passed in the United Kingdom that came to be known as the Alan Turing law, which retroactively pardoned men convicted for outlawed homosexual acts.

"Turing Tested": Turing's 1952 article "The Chemical Basis of Morphogenesis" describes how natural features such as spots and spirals arise from a homogenous state. These are now called Turing patterns. The notion of contrary sensations as a description of same-sex desire is drawn from Karl Westphal's diagnosis described in "Contrary Sexual Feeling" or "die conträre Sexualempfindung" (1870). Westphal is a central figure of 19th-century sexology, credited with one of the first medical accounts of sexuality as a psychiatric disorder giving way to the "discovery" of male homosexuality.

Some of the biographic details of this section are owed to David Leavitt's *The Man Who Knew Too Much* (2006). Some details are also fictionalized. The collection's eponymous line, "No doubt I will return a different man," is adapted from a letter Turing sent just prior to his final ordeal: "I've now got myself into the kind of trouble that I have always considered to be quite a possibility for me... I shall shortly be pleading guilty to a charge of sexual offences with a young man. The story of how it all came to be found out is a long and fascinating one, which I shall have to make into a short story one day, but haven't the time to tell you now. No doubt I shall emerge from it all a different man, but quite who I've not found out."

"Some Broken Colossus": This poem takes its start from Jorge Luis Borges's short story "The Circular Ruins" (translated by Andrew Hurley), particularly the lines, "Not to be a man, to be the projection of another man's dream, what a feeling of humiliation, of vertigo! All fathers are interested in the children they have procreated (they have permitted to exist) in mere confusion or pleasure..."

"Sonata for One Clarinet by John Cage": "Sonata for Clarinet" is an early work of Cage's, composed in 1933. It is also known under the title "Sonata for One Voice." There are three movements: Vivace, Lento, and Vivace.

"I Propose to Reconsider the Question": To begin his 1950 landmark paper "Computing Machinery and Intelligence," Turing writes: "I PROPOSE to consider the question, 'Can machines think?' This should begin with definitions of the meaning of the terms 'machine' and 'think'. The definitions might be framed so as to reflect so far as possible the normal use of the words, but this attitude is dangerous. If the meaning of the words 'machine' and 'think' are to be found by examining how they are commonly used it is difficult to escape the conclusion that the meaning and the answer to the question, 'Can machines think?' is to be sought in a statistical survey such as a Gallup poll. But this is absurd. Instead of attempting such a definition I shall replace the question by another, which is closely related to it and is expressed in relatively unambiguous words." Immediately after this Turing describes the "imitation game," a systematic way to determine kinds of intelligence, whether human or machine, what is later called the Turing Test.

ACKNOWLEDGMENTS

My gratitude to these journals for their publication and support, where some of these poems have appeared under different titles or in different forms: *Academy of American Poets, The Arkansas International, Bellingham Review, Blackbird, The Georgia Review, Meridian, Mid-American Review, Mississippi Review, Split This Rock, Spoon River Poetry Review, Texas Review,* and *Third Coast.*

To my beautiful teachers, Kimberly Blaeser, Michael Dennis Browne, Brenda Cárdenas, Michael Heffernan, Davis McCombs, G.E. Patterson, and Alexandra Teague, thanks for believing. Every moment in your company was essential.

For their decisive guidance, I am most indebted to Geoffrey Brock and Rebecca Dunham. Your time and attention became this book.

For all the finishing touches, endless gratitude to the CSU Poetry Center crew, especially to the brilliant Caryl Pagel. And to Randall Mann, ever elegant and insightful, thanks for finding merit here and giving these words a stage. And special thanks to the wonderful Brian Blanchfield and Paisley Rekdal for their generosity.

To every attentive reader and workshop comrade, for every spark, thank you, but most especially Kara van de Graaf, Soham Patel, Michael McGriff, Zach Carlsen, John Myers, Matthew Shrode Hargis, Sherri Hoffman, Ching-In Chen, Brittany Cavallaro, Michael Walsh, Jacob Shores-Argüello, Chloe Honum, Rebecca Hazelton, Ashley Anna McHugh, and Jen Jabaily-Blackburn. Word magicians, all.

Love to Will Clements and Rochelle Smith for reigniting belief in the concept of a muse. And to my dearest Mary Angelino, what a gift to write alongside you.

To my mother and sister, all beauty is maternal thanks to you. Your permission and your guiding light made this possible, and your strength.

And to the men who saw me across every finish line: in so many ways, you gave space for these poems to exist. I love you still.

RECENT CLEVELAND STATE UNIVERSITY POETRY CENTER PUBLICATIONS

Edited by Caryl Pagel & Hilary Plum

POETRY

World'd Too Much: The Selected Poetry of Russell Atkins ed. Kevin Prufer and
    Robert E. McDonough
Advantages of Being Evergreen by Oliver Baez Bendorf
Dream Boat by Shelley Feller
My Fault by Leora Fridman
Orient by Nicholas Gulig
Twice There Was A Country by Alen Hamza
Age of Glass by Anna Maria Hong
In One Form to Find Another by Jane Lewty
50 Water Dreams by Siwar Masannat
daughterrarium by Sheila McMullin
The Bees Make Money in the Lion by Lo Kwa Mei-en
Residuum by Martin Rock
Festival by Broc Rossell
Sun Cycle by Anne Lesley Selcer
Arena by Lauren Shapiro
Bottle the Bottles the Bottles the Bottles by Lee Upton

ESSAYS

I Liked You Better Before I Knew You So Well by James Allen Hall
A Bestiary by Lily Hoang
Codependence by Amy Long
The Leftovers by Shaelyn Smith

TRANSLATIONS

Scorpionic Sun by Mohammed Khaïr-Eddine, translated by Conor Bracken
I Burned at the Feast: Selected Poems of Arseny Tarkovsky translated by Philip Metres
    and Dimitri Psurtsev

For a complete list of titles visit www.csupoetrycenter.com

Tobias Wray is a poet of the American South and Midwest. His writing has appeared in various journals, including *Blackbird, Bellingham Review, Meridian, Third Coast, Wasafiri: International Contemporary Writing, Spoon River Poetry Review, Hunger Mountain*, and *The Georgia Review*. Some of his poems have been featured in anthologies, including *The Queer Nature Anthology* (Autumn House Press) and *The Queer Movement Anthology of Literatures* (Seagull Books). He served as a poetry editor for *Cream City Review* at the University of Wisconsin-Milwaukee and holds an MFA in Poetry and Translation from the University of Arkansas.